DONETSK INTERVAL

DONETSK INTERVAL

Dennis Marden Clark

WAKING LION PRESS

ISBN 978-1-4341-0421-2

The views expressed in this book are the responsibility of the
author and do not necessarily represent the position of the
publisher.

Published by Waking Lion Press, an imprint of The Editorium.
Waking Lion Press™, the Waking Lion Press logo, and The
Editorium™ are trademarks of The Editorium, LLC.

The Editorium, LLC
West Jordan City, UT 84081-6132
wakinglionpress.com
wakinglion@editorium.com

Contents

Preface

Valerie and I applied for missionary service at the Heber Valley Girls' Camp in November of 2006. We called the President of that mission after hearing a couple report, in Sacrament Meeting, on their mission to the camp. We submitted our application and he requested us and we started looking into four-wheelers — we had to provide our own — and sent in our sizes for the mission jackets. We were certain we were going, despite our Bishop's having asked us three times during our interview "But will you go where you are called?" We answered "Yes, but please say that we want to serve in the Heber Valley Girls' Camp."

I should have known that something was up when our Stake President asked the same question, and we gave the same answer. That was in February, 2007. In April Valerie got a letter asking her to have a mammogram, which she did. A day or two later, the President of the Heber Valley mission called and asked had we heard anything? We told him about the letter. He said "You're not coming here. Our missionaries don't need medical exams. I'm looking for someone else."

And he was right. A week later we got a letter asking us to serve in the Ukraine Donetsk Mission. We said okay, and started with the vaccination sequences designed to prepare us for that part of Ukraine. We finished the sequence as we exhausted the Russian lessons we could get at the MTC, and then we flew out to Donetsk, via Wien. I started writing poems almost as soon as we arrived, although the prelude and postlude poems were written before we arrived, and after we returned home, respectively. I hope you find something to like in these pages.

PRELUDE

what rock & water say

What Rock Says to Water

Stay. Stop and play.
Here, in this wash, be still.
Wait a week. Keep me wet.
Stand in the sand. Stick with these stones.
I look in your face and find my own.
Back when I flew, we danced and flung
ourselves against an older ground,
picking, flushing, scraping, prying.
That was before I settled:
shallow sea, sandy bed.
Wait at the foot of this wall. Pool.
At bedrock lie and braid with me.

water answers rock

i'll warm with you, and you
come run with me
leaping boulders
i'll be tears for your face
while it thaws
we can tumble seaward, slopping
grinding stones, flinging logs,
slipping, seeping
we'll cut our way through

the sad sediments
scour the graves
scoop out and roll the old bones
when I leave you sunk with them
in a bowl of slickrock
don't sink too deep
i'll be back and we can flee
further, a little further

OPENING EXERCISES

Miners' Day, 2007

It's Miners' Day — Donetsk is built on coal —
and fireworks set off the car alarms.
Sixteen years back Ukraine reclaimed its soul,
scything itself from Russia — not by arms
but ballot taking back its mines and farms.

They made less of that anniversary —
last Friday's fireworks were more subdued.
Tonight they tunnel through the sky and free
the spark and smoke that hang like miners' fruit
and drift across the city and its mood.

A mine collapsed in Utah just before
we came here. Now its owner has declared
memorial and tomb forevermore
the tunnels where six miners in their merde
guttered, drowning in their last breath, and scared —

and three who dug to free them and were killed
when coal and stone collapsed and crushed their lungs.
That way inspection won't disturb their chilled,
congealed blood — and not dissuade their sons
from climbing down the owner's rotten rungs.

No Miners' Day in Utah. In Ukraine
the fireworks explode like coal-bed gas,
the shattered night falls like a burning rain,
a herald of the next mining disaster
when methane and a chisel have a blast.

The independent government will open
an inquiry and call for safer mines
until the families, who are always hoping,
are numbed again by poverty, and lines
form for the jobs created by the fines.

For Donetsk, 2007

I sing Donetsk, laid out on a grid by a Welshman over the
  rolling hills of Ukraine,
imprinted with roads like the impression of screen wire on
  the rind of a cheese —
by John James Hughes, of Wales, importing for some Tsar
  or other an entire industry
to make rails and steel plate, for his attempted railroads and
  an attempt at launching
warships for his own warm-water Black Sea Fleet, one to
  show muscle to the entire world.
I sing John Hughes, sailing in 1870 with the entire
  steelworks, and the workers from London,
who laid out Yuzovska, home for miners and ironworkers —
  a favor returned by the Donyechyani
who have remodeled a back alley in honor of Great Britain,
  with a stage for the Beatles,
from Liverpool, cast in bronze from their Cavern Club days,
  welcoming strollers
to an alley filled with restaurants, clothing stores, shops,
  and a climbing wall,
where the young of Donetsk try to get a grip on the reality
  of the city that spawned them.

Yuzovska of the Donbas, displacing with its furnaces and
  pit-heads the village of Oleksandrivka,
named for a different Tsar before 1799, regardless of the
  wishes of the Cossacks who lived there,
Yuzovska, in turn renamed Stalino when the sons of Hughes
  fled with their families to Wales
after the Bolshevik revolution, after filling its mines with

Russian moles sniffing out coal
in the limestone, fuel to smelt the iron ore also mined in the
    Donbas, and the gas discovered in 1934 —
the year after sewers were first sunk into the streets — the
    exploitation of all these resources I sing,
a pursuit that leaves the bedrock beneath the city so full of
    tunnels, pockets and cavities
that trains roll into the city at half-speed to avoid collapsing
    the whole wheel of cheese.
Stalino, which as an industrial center escaped starvation
    when the farms were collectivized
and the kulaks shipped to Siberia on rails of its making. The
    city that now sighs in the night
with the rumble of coal into railcars — destroyed in the
    Great Patriotic War and rebuilt by the tsar
Dzhugashvili, and after his death renamed for the Seversky
    Donets, tributary to the great river Don.

Self-proclaimed capital of that river basin drenched in
    Ukrainian, Russian and German blood,
shattered by blitzkrieg and patched up by the Nazis to hold
    their herded Jews, Poles, Czechs:
ghetto and concentration camp, stuffed with over 100,000
    Roma, Sinti, Jehovah's Witnesses,
Communist, Freemason, homeless, beggar, mentally ill and
    other "subhuman" corpses,
adding to the concentration of natural gas in the soil that
    sometimes bubbles and sighs.
Rebuilt in Soviet concrete, and Soviet until wise fools
    allowed the Ukrainian people to vote
on their preference for further exploitation by Russia, and
    they chose to fly their own flag instead,

blue above for the heavens that weep for Ukrainian
    peasants starved in the collectivization,
yellow below for the fields of grain ripening on the blood
    and bone of generations of
Cimmerians, Scythians, Bulgars, Jews, Goths, Khazars,
    Tatars, Cossacks, Lithuanians, Poles,
Turkmen — and the armies who have tried to conquer the
    land: Russians, Frenchmen, half a league
of Englishmen, Austro-Hungarians, Germans hunting
    Lebensraum for das Herrenvolk —
and the rest who have fought over this land without
    understanding that it doesn't belong to anyone
but God and the peasants buried among their fields and all
    of the slaughtered innocents
and, in Donetsk, the miners, the shocktyore, whose tombs
    lie in rubble beneath the city's rind.

I sing the beautiful women, slender and fair, who strut the
    streets on spike heels sharp enough
to drive through the helmets and into the brains of the next
    soldiers who try to destroy their city,
of the men who drive as if their cars were T-3 tanks from
    Kharkiv to the north,
who polish their cars in the morning after a rain, with
    chamois and bucket, scouring off the dust
of heavy metals spewed into the air at the coal-mines where
    rock is crushed to rubble
and the hills of slag continue to grow like dolmens ringing
    the city, sporting trees like a comb-over,
of lakes gathered in sinkholes and draining into one
    another until they meander on to the sea of Azov,
one last gathering of Donbas waters before they flow into

the Black Sea, & Mediterranean, & are lost,
of men who stroll along the streets at dusk, their hands
 around the slender brown necks
of beer bottles, drinking their freedom and the liberty of the
 city and their land before the next
conqueror I sing, I who have come to this city from the
 deserts of America to preach a new Jerusalem.

I sing Donetsk brutal and rough, a pockmarked face on the
 steppe, rebuilding itself behind concrete
faced with Ukrainian brick — exposed and weathering,
 concealing the quarters being remodeled,
apartments being improved by people who will not leave
 because they are the city's,
who look to Russia and Poland like Janus, two-faced,
 suspicious of Armenian, Nigerian, Mongolian
students in their universities, fearing, like Americans, that
 these new faces will rub theirs in the dirt,
who cling to that climbing wall belayed, whose city is in
 their blood like lead and vanadium,
like that grimy Atlantic port that spawned music which
 shook Hamburg, then London, then the world.

Postscript, 2014

When they poured across the border, the Russians came in
 mufti, little green men without insignia,
to take back the Crimean Peninsula that they stole from the
 Ottoman Empire — and the Tatars,
whom Stalin also exiled to Vorkuta — Russians coming to
 steal once more from Ukraine,

a former Soviet Socialist Republic, to whom Kruschev, born
   in Ukraine, deeded the peninsula,
proving that you can't trust a Russian — though none of the
   Russians dressed as babushkas.
They came as a militia, self-directed, mere citizens in
   another Olympic contest, bringing the Sochi spirit
to a new war game, and without instigation from Putin, no
   drug testing needed;
and what drug would we test Putin for? Hubris? Hubbub?
   Hugger-mugger?
And when the peninsula was liberated and its freedom
   secured and its peoples subdued,
they came for Donetsk — invited by the hunger of the
   Donétskaya Naródnaya Respúblika, —
they always come in the name of the people, act in the
   name of liberation, the conquerors.
They were fighters on furlough said Putin, free men fighting
   for the freedom of all Russians everywhere!
The people I know from Donetsk, some moved to Kyiv,
   where they settled into a new life —
some stayed in the city, unable to get out; others were
   happy to be liberated from the Orange Revolution.

Postscript, 2022

When they poured across the border, one squadron aimed
   for Chernobyl, and its Ukrainian guards,
Ukrainians tasked with keeping people safe and out of
   Prypyat, the atomic city, and harm's way,
and after hours of heavy fighting, the Russians took back
   Prypyat, a Soviet prize!

When they roared across the border, it was not for room
   and board —
those they intended to destroy — but to bring death and
   disorder, conquest and civilization;
and when their victims rose from the ashes with fire-
   bottles, slugs and clubs,
they were not fighting for a new world order but the old
   disorder —
messy, inconstant, contingent — that freedom requires to
   thrive.
The more things change, the more that stays the same, sad
   to say.
When Russian forces struck at a ravine in the center of Kyiv
was it to annihilate Titova's, Bazhan's and Yevtushenko's
   poems,
or the broadcast tower? They failed at both, like kicking an
   own goal with a bald ball.
Leaving us to wonder what drug Putin should be tested for
   this time,
and how will he respond to the needle drawing blood . . .

Старейшина (Star-y-a-shena)

The root of this Russian word,
"to stand," shares that sense
with its cousin in Latin, its cognate
in "stare decisis." A stacking
of stone on stone to raise
a tower, a house, a tomb —
star-y-a-shena, my title —
careful stress constructing
tomorrow's ruins. It means
"elder," oldster, a geezer
standing, still, and staring.

Moroni 11

For five days I lay among the dead,
hidden by corpses from the Lamanites
who sought the wounded on the field of battle
about Cumorah, coming to kill and plunder.
Nights I wormed myself under the dead.
That did not mean they wouldn't find and kill me.
They speared and hacked at every body they could
until the stench of death drove them away.
Then I wormed my way into Cumorah.

Mormon, my father, had sent a letter before
the battle, instructing me to finish his work,
and that includes abridging the record of Ether.
Now he is dead, and I have no more gold
nor copper to make plates for such a task.

As I thus sat, attempting to follow Mormon's
last directives, knowing my world destroyed,
and feeling shattered in my solitude,
despairing I would live to finish that,
I heard the breathing of a writhing man
entering Cumorah through the cave
that twists and like a serpent in the stone
disgorges one who has the faith to follow
into the pyramid, against all fear —
one of the Three who tarried. I was stunned.

"So, I am sent to bring you out, Moroni.
Leave these glowing stones. Come to the sun.
We have a world to show you, whole and sane.

Come to the sun and see. You can return
to follow Mormon's dictates once you're whole
again." He took me by the hand and tugged —
I could but follow him out through the traps.

The other two were waiting, standing guard,
and when we set the final hiding stone,
and came out of the cave, and slipped into
the shadows, a stench of death still guarded this,
the place of final slaughter of our armies
though none of Laman's horde patrolled the place —
they were out hunting down the ones who fled,
which made it simpler for us to get away.

They led me southward, whither my people fled,
southward and westward, into the setting sun,
heading towards a sea where Lamanites
would not expect to see us traveling, if
they hunted us at all. I fretted that
the Three might leave me as I slept, and so
I slept but little, only to wake and find
them near. We moved by day, but still we kept
to shadows on the trails of animals,
avoiding paths and traders' roads, traversing
settled areas only at night, escaping
notice as best we could, eating what came
to hand, and slowly, softly, reached the sea.

The Three had been directed by the Lord
to leave the land when wars began again
and wickedness destroyed the love of friends —
and now the unity of war was fraying,

the Lamanites were starting to slay each other —
the Three had come to rescue me from war.
They'd left before, in search of Hagoth's folk,
who'd left in a large ship four hundred years
before. But when we reached the sea, no ship:
they had a planked canoe hidden ashore.

"We found more peoples up along the coast
than Hagoth's — and none answered to that name.
One people taught us how to build this boat,
and paddle in the sea. They call themselves
Chumash, and they hunt and trade in peace."
And here we paused to lift and launch the craft,
hauling it down the beach as best we could,
and going back with branches to erase
our tracks, though none lived near that we could see.

We climbed into the boat just as we were.
"We'll find our food along the way," they said.
"You sit up front," they said, and handed me
a tree leaf made of wood. "Reach forward there,
and push it in, and pull it back towards you.
Another people called the Natinook-wa
live on rivers up among giant trees,
making canoes from fallen trunks burnt out —
and though they trade with rival folk, they also
live at peace with them. We will take you
to visit with them, live among them, learn —
as you will learn to paddle on the sea."

Thus we set out and worked. Within a week,
camping on beaches, eating from sea and land,

paddling all day long, not often seeing
anyone, we'd reached a calmer place,
where, looking down, we saw Leviathan
suckling her pup like any mother and child,
sometimes surfacing to spray us with
their breath, then diving — as if the ocean breathed.
I wanted to stay, but though we camped ashore
and went back several days to see that sight,
the Three would not that we should linger there,
despite the serpent rock that guarded us
where we would turn again into the rough.

We left and paddled into wilder waters.
Coasting northwards, we began again
to paddle, now with double-bladed leaves
toiling all day, sunup to sundown, stopping
to drink at every stream, and fill our bladders,
picking among the plants that grew there, greeting
any who lived there, though there were but few,
and none at all who greeted us with spears.
We came one evening to an island off
the coast, steered by the Third onto a strand,
and climbed a cleft in the cliff to its flat top.
"See this" he said, gesturing at a bush,
and in the fading light I saw a snake,
coiled beneath its limbs, illuminated
by the dying light. "This is our meal"
he said, and stooping and singing took the snake
and held it up for us to see its length
and heft, holding it behind the head, and humming.
"Moroni, take your knife, cut off its head."
The other two were busy sparking fire.

"But first, you thank the snake for being here
to feed us, even though it has not fed."
I drew my knife and knelt and said "I thank you,
O snake, for being here to feed the four
of us as we are traveling to the north,
although you have not eaten yet today.
For though you came as on the wings of eagles,
or swam the swells of ocean to arrive,
we honor you" — and I sawed off its head
with my sharp flint. We gutted the snake and coiled
it round the fire to roast, its rattles drooping
into the flames where we had set its head.
The meat was welcome, as a change from fish,
although I woke that night to rattling fears.

Thus we moved on, meeting the Chumash first,
whose boats the Three had modeled their boat on,
though not so colorful. They showed us how
to spear the dolphin, which could feed us all
for weeks, and tried to teach their dolphin dance.
I danced with feet like flippers, and fell down.
Moving on north, and hunting as we went,
we traded dolphin with the Ex'seien
for acorn bread and flour — they'd use the skins
for boats to fish from — and we paddled north.

The Three were taking me to where three peoples
lived peaceably enough — the Natinook-wa,
the Arra-arra and the Olekwo'l, all
along two rivers. When they went to sea,
fishing for salmon, they brought back and traded
among themselves the bounty of water and land.

And every year they danced to firm the earth,
with a white deerskin dance, and jumping dance,
and many who were wealthy in skins sponsored
the dancers, though only the Olekwo'l
claimed to own the land, bought it and sold.
I saw these peoples live in peace, and care
for their poor, and love their mother earth,
and I was saddened for the Lamanites.

When next we moved, again in our planked boat,
we moved back south into a bay almost
as large as where we'd seen Leviathan.
We paddled up a river many days
among the Mewuk, who most welcomed us,
and Wintun. On that river, we found peace,
until the Three showed me a place where gold
and copper could be found in placid curves,
where rushing rivers slowed. I tried to show
the Mewuk how I could make from those ores,
heating and hammering, heating and hammering
upon a quern long used to grind acorns
and nuts and other seeds, of fit dimensions,
and after the hammering, heating and smoothing
until my labors left me with a leaf,
a leaf that flexed like bark but would not split
nor crimp. "We call that ziff," I told the people,
but they preferred their tightly woven baskets
with flared-out sides, and had no use for gold.
So for a year I worked at making plates,
melting, hammering, smoothing them with stones
while the Three hunted, gathered, fished and talked
with Mewuk and with Wintun, people who

laughed as my leaves gave up their golden sheen.
I told them where we came from we had fruits
that I could use to polish off the patina
they found amusing, sheum and neas, which
we also ate. I passed a year that way.

The Three instructed Mewuk and Wintun men
in how to follow the river to the sea,
and paddle back again up to their homes.
We left the boat for them, and walked away
among new peoples, living on little water,
bearing south, and where we went, the Three
were welcomed by folk whose languages they'd learned
in earlier travels. After months of walking,
while I got used to packing plates on my back,
we crossed a mighty river red with mud
and walked into a desert where its peoples
lived at peace and shared a different river
that ran between two knotted heaps of mountains,
using its water to raise their food, as we,
the Nephites and the Lamanites, had done
once, in peace, before my father's father's
days. I wept for that and mourned again.

The Three were welcomed, honored as sages here,
and one of the maidens asked about my weeping.
They told the story of my people's wars,
how I escaped the slaughter, but had seen
my father, mother, brothers, sisters, slain,
and though we fought, my own contingent slain,
and how I must return and write that record.
She tried to comfort me, and from her face,

and how the Three translated what she said,
I knew her grace was real enough, and I
accepted it and thanked her, and from that
grew love. I learned a little of her tongue
and we stayed long enough for me to wed,
and as a dowry I gave her all the gold
I had not fashioned into plates, and all
the copper likewise. We knew I would leave,
but now I had a place to come back to.

When I had held our firstborn for a month
we left, the Three and I; my load was light,
my steps were quicker, they were happier,
and thus alert we made our cautious way
back to Cumorah, where I polished up
the plates. The Three brought food to me as I
began the work of finishing Mormon's record,
abridging the record Ether had bequeathed
to us, lit by his stones. When I was thus
engaged, and had a store of food laid by,
the Three adjudged me whole, and went away
to search out other folk and offer hope.

True

The tire bears the weight of your full mass,
cushions you from the pavement or the trail,
warms as it flexes, squirms at every turn,
protects the tube of air that steers your speed —
but it's the wheel that keeps the tire true.

The wheel spins on bearings at its hub,
lubed with a heavy grease to spread the heat
and keep the hub and axle just enough
apart that even through the longest ride
it keeps the metal kiss ardent but cool.

But it's the spokes that keep the wheel true;
each pulls the rim against its partner's pull,
keeping it centered in the fork between
the brake pads as it races, on a roll,
to bear you where you think you want to be.

The spokes that flex, deform, to hold the path,
are screwed with nipples to the rim. They move
and bend and twist with every torque and fluke.
Slipping, catching they twist against the rim,
each slowly losing hold of flexing spoke.

They must be tightened constantly, in pairs,
to bring the spokes to tension, each one tight
against its neighbor's pull the other way,
pulling the rim from right and left to center,
to make each rim run true between the forks.

When Jesus Spoke

When Jesus spoke in Bountiful,
He first said "Come and feel
The wounds that killing left on me,
And how our God can heal.

"I call you now to witness this,
My body in its flesh,
And with this bread commemorate
It's been created fresh,

"And with this water witness that
Although my blood was shed,
I stand among you whole again,
Released from that stone bed."

Father in Heaven

What more that name than a wish my father were dead?
A father in heaven, further away from my life,
impacting events described to the easily led —
not hand on butt nor voice in air I breathed.
Had Freud not poisoned the lit I took and read —
the books he taught — we'd still have shared our strife —
If we're Œdipus wrecks Freud cut the brake lines and fled.

By the time we could walk together discussing Pound,
when he'd reprove and I no longer seethed,
and we worked side by side harrowing ground
down garden and he'd helped me choose a wife,
I left, pursuing learning in the round
of classes, papers, tests and grades that wreathed
certification by degrees, and found

myself four times a father, being taught
how sharper than et cetera is the knife
a son can use to carve away all thought
from nerve and muscle. Now that I have teethed
on anger, now that I know where he got
the impulse to pop his dentures and drool at life,
I think I may know demons he might've fought.

His death is no exaggerated rumor
although I wasn't there when his blood seethed
with oxygen. He wasn't a consumer
of fear of death. He loved and left his wife,
she says, the muse who nurtured this late bloomer.
I wish I had a father in heaven wreathed
in sweat, with false teeth and a sense of humor.

Warpaint

I daub it on by finger, gelled and blue,
to skin still wet with tears. I rub — it foams.
I'm after partisans — persistent, too,
rebels who can't let go their ground, their homes
in the wilderness of my face. I squint. I cut
them down with five blades to my scythe and toss
their dead remains and wash my blades off, but
they surface yet again. They brook no loss
like loss of face, and right under my nose.
I've harrowed this field so often it should erode.
I knock myself out, but if it came to blows
I'd suffer big time, reaping what I've sowed.
It's just a fake beard, digitally applied,
that lures me to cure my face by scraping hide.

Setting

We built this deck so we could sit out, watch
the sun set, your Daddy and me. That's why
we built into the hill, to get this view.

You know, we had the architect occident
the house so we could see across the lake.
Somebody else had started a house here but
ran out of money. We bought a used-house lot.

All these mountains, I feel I'm so hemmed in.
A bowl of mountains, but cracked by Provo Canyon.
I thought you'd locked me in with all those deadbolts.

There are deer down in the garden. They come in
over the fence from the student housing — there —
and bed down in the weeds where Dad grew corn.
I wish he'd come get me. I'm tired of waiting.

That tree has apricots this year, but not
a bee. How did they get themselves pollinated?
Funny how fruit will find a way, then freeze.

Don't I have a son named Kevin? Isn't
he your brother? You used to call him your "little
bother" when you were trying to train him, but
it was you who bothered him. That's what I saw.

It's burning across the lake, that mountain there,
the one they're building all the houses on.
The lights get in the way, rectangled up.

Do you remember the little black rabbit eating
all the flowers off the graves? Bury me
next to Dad, and maybe put in a bench
where you can watch the sun set over the lake.

Crunching Numbers

For Diane Bradshaw, in London H.Q., at the end of the email line

Like you, I'm crunching numbers all day long.

So far, they're shattered and scattered all over the floor,
flung from the keyboard where I pound away.

Shards of the shells that litter my desk like paper,
though sharp enough to cut the careless hand,
invite the eye to read the history
of all my work, and that's a good thing, for
if I got up to walk I'd step on one,
and I can't bear to hear the poor things squeal.

Sometimes they pop. A ruptured three emits
miasma of despair that hugs the floor,
concealing all the other liberated
numerals, while a seven, broken, squirms,
a little snake whose venom smells like loss.

I've never squished a dual-chambered eight
and so can only guess what it contains,
but six and nine are musk and ambergris —
sharper than anything refined for scent,
both hard to open and harder still to close.
And ones are honed harpoons, and work their way
into the calloused skin that caps my heel,
hard to remove and harder to leave alone.

I always prefer an open four — who knows what
the little trap conceals? or what, once swallowed,
it does inside your stomach as it thaws?
I wash my hands when I've been calculating
just to avoid that sure and sudden knowledge.
And two and five, fraternal twins, might come
unhinged from being trodden on, so if

I have to stand and walk away, I hope
it's zero my foot finds first, to nullify

the suffering my crunching always causes.

Душа моя! = Dusha moya!

Often printed in English hymnals as "Be Still, My Soul"

They sang Душа моя! in church today.
When I first learned this song, I sang "This is
my land" to Jean Sibelius's music.
My land was central Utah, and high desert —
though not a howling wilderness, because
the Mormon settlers who displaced the Utes,
plowing and sowing where they had gathered seed,
who fenced where they had roamed, and brought the cow
where pronghorns leapt and mulies browsed all day,
enjoyed their seven years of plenty for
ten times that long before the desert howled.
Damming the streams for irrigation, these
quick pioneers spread thinly all that melted
and all that mountains milked from passing clouds.
No longer persecuted for their faith,
nor hunted as cohabs by federal marshals,
my parents' parents suffered the Depression —
and dry years and poor crops — but not the pen;
my parents fought the second World War
from Hollywood, where my father worked for Lockheed,
and I was born in hospital, not at home;
then I was singing hymns to peace and freedom
and slaughtering Lloyd Stones' "This is my song".

I learned that song when Mormon Democratic
progressive politics were morphing into
the hard McCarthyist intolerance
my parents' great-grandparents found coiled up

in Illinois, Missouri and Ohio
when they were poor and only had the ballot
as currency wherever they tried to settle,
and couldn't buy a single politician.
When Joseph Smith was running for president
as Democrat and abolitionist,
Republicans had not yet organized,
nor trumpeted to life inveighing on
the twin relics of barbarism — slavery
and Mormon polygamy — and by the time
Old Abe had sent Orion Clemens west,
instructed to sound Brigham Young about
the Mormons, whether they'd support the Union,
the Anti-Bigamy Act of '62
was more than just a gleam in Morrill's eye.

So there I was, a hundred odd years later,
on Hallowe'en in 1962
out Trick or Treating for UNICEF, and asking
spare change for children's health throughout the world,
and hearing from the ghouls who opened doors
the U.N. was a vast left-wing conspiracy
to strip America of sovereignty
and bring us under a godless socialist
Soviet one-world control — and so, today,
while I sit in a chapel in Ukraine
and hear that tune by Jean Sibelius,
a quiet moment from Finlandia
I'd learned years later as "Be still my soul,"
sung by a Belarusian, a Ukrainian,
an American, in the tongue of the Soviets,
I smiled at how the plot can't help but thicken.

Renovations

First thing the Donyechani did
when they got title to their apartments in
the dissolution of the Soviet Union:
replace the wooden door frames with steel frames
and steel doors, with five deadbolts to shoot
into the frame, to keep visitors out.

The second renovation was new windows,
double- or triple-glazed in wooden frames,
to keep in winter heat from civic boilers,
to keep out summer heat from sun-hot clouds.
No windows were harmed in placing of air conditioners —
they put them through the walls, and kept their views.

The third change was to enclose the balconies —
on the north, as a barrier to winter's cold;
on the south, as a place to dry their laundry;
on the east, a place to smoke naked in the dawn;
on the west, to watch the nightly fireworks —
and sometimes, in any direction, another bed.

Or lacking a balcony, install a water
filter system — City water — kitchen sink.
We use three filters: one for heavy metals;
one for viruses and germs in water;
one for the grit, and flakes of rust from the pipes —
that one you change when nothing flows any more.

We see these "remonts" walking around Donetsk —
looking at our own Shekspira trinadzat,

at older tetraplexes, and 40-flat risers —
especially the brand new construction everywhere:
the one-legged cranes that rotate to watch us pass
the mansions mixing with dachas and pensions.

Donetsk Crows

I'd like to take a picture of the crows
that flew into Donetsk in mid-October
but when I focus they refuse to pose,
unlike the pigeons, who are far less sober —

the crows will only croak once they're alarmed;
the pigeons coo and burble all the time,
assembling at the dumpsters while, forearmed,
the crows flip off and scatter, flap and climb,

until they reach a branch they think is safe,
and eye me as I pass. Pigeons divide —
Red Sea of brooding blood — and later strafe
my windows, pooping, aiming for inside.

These crows don't give a damn, don't want to roost
inside my cave, don't gather at the garbage,
to peck at bottles, looking to get juiced,
but prod the duff for nuts in this day's forage.

The crows have landed on a longer flight,
summoned by shorter days to minister
an end to Autumn, stay until the night
shortens again — nothing more sinister.

Stepping in habit fit for fall, and sober,
meet for a portrait since they struck that pose
and flew into Donetsk in mid-October —
I'd like to take a picture of these crows.

Theology of Evolution

When God is done digesting me, and shits
the husk, I pray you leave what's left alone.
When I shit in the woods, a six-inch hole
suffices to receive and bury all.
Atop the plot a stone won't keep the mice,
the jays, the squirrels, from sickening on the spoils.
What need embalming, stone and six-foot hole
for what remains of me? A platform in
some limbs, a Parsee tower. Allow my breath
now stilled, now silent, the joy and honor of
the voice of vultures, eagles, jays and crows,
of bears and boars and flies — of all who will.
And let the feast be one for them of many,
and may they then go scuff through cemeteries,
perch or squat on stones with passing haste,
excrete what's indigestible, and go
after the next and next meal, till the last.

Хорошо 広島市 (Horosho Hiroshima)

. . . he was a horrorshow filthy fighter
and very handy with the boot . . .
— Anthony Burgess, A Clockwork Orange

Thank God for the atom bomb
— Paul Fussell

We had but three and one we threw
away, and dropped the other two
when drunk on blood and driving drugged —
we flicked our butts and off we flew,

our windows down, our music up.
We gunned the engine, geared that pup
through five, laid rubber, really bugged
the broads — hell, that bitter cup

we almost hurled, we laughed so hard,
turned cat's asses in our own front yard
and shot off shit-faced, shredded, thugged —
we shaved our boils with a shard

sitting in isolation cells
suffering personal, private hells
feeling slapped around and slugged
in cold so deep it froze our yells.

But this is now and that was then:
we'd never shoot that shit again —
get shredded while the world shrugged —
we were just boys, but now we're men.

Necktie Party

Ties are my pantyhose — unnecessary
item of clothing which I would not wear
if not required attire for the office
I hold — vestigial latter-day livery
which suits me as a noose the shivery
ghosts of Tower of London, whom the sophist
considers an outward sigh of inward fear
rather than remnant of a bloody Mary.

Borne as the laver he carried to shave face
from stairhead to parapet, gently I carry
the one I will wear — or the one that will wear me,
mark of my shavery to one who gave grace.
White shirt, dark suit, black sox — all complement
the tie that marks me as a penitent.

Unorthodox

So Christmas in Ukraine is Orthodox.
The Julian calendar now has it fall
some 13 days after the western feast,
so here in Donetsk we welcome Christmas twice:
the one we brought from Utah — which, though nice,
is mission work — and this one with its priest.
Strewn across the stone we fill the hall
of the Cathedral, where one babushka rocks,
crossing and bowing (as the priest incants),
more than the young, whose dutiful bow and cross
partake more of the dancer than the dance,
and I stand here unbowing, feel the loss
of priests who sing the scriptures with pure feeling,
and hidden choirs who haunt the vaulted ceiling.

Ukrainian mud

The rain brings wave on wave
of dirty water,
for Donetsk cannot pave
itself enough —
no matter who might slave —
mostly some man's daughter
set out, enrolled, to stave
off the stuff,
to stop the flow of mud
mixed with Ukrainian blood.

It does not cling but clot
on shoe and cuff
like mucilaginous snot
refreshed by rain,
so every splash and spot
is stout enough
to stick before you blot —
you host the stain,
can't stop the flow, of mud
mixed with Ukrainian blood.

It works into the weave,
like bone-deep pain,
of leg and sock and sleeve —
empire's daughter —
no brush can make it leave —
mark of the slain —
just spread it, make it cleave
firmer, broader —
not stop the flow of mud
mixed with Ukrainian blood.

Plural Marriage

Like any Mormon man I've married many
a woman in my life. In what is left
I'll marry more — I plan on many now.
They're all alive. No serial polyg –
some weeks I've slept with one a night, herself
electing, or us letting luck decide,
some weeks with one companion for the week.
More men should wed more women. Works for us.

I've married many women. All of them
dwell in a single body: Vallory
(a spelling she regarded as a spell
to keep her, Utah-fashion, name unique).
The surfer girl who posed in her bikini
was fading when we met, and in her place
the English, French and German student blossomed,
and, while I went off in pastoral exile
to Texas, chose her languages and major —
and wrote me letters any missionary
would love — about her studies, work, vacations
(three avocations she pursued together
in Salzburg, a semester spent abroad,
and whence to London, thence Stratford — and home).
A grad student when I returned from Texas,
a teacher of composition who had learned
that teaching discomposed her, she still taught
me to love Tolkien, newly published here,
Austen, whose enthusiastic acolyte
she stood as, and herself, and middle Beatles.
We got engaged and I flew off to Salzburg

to study abroad — I studied several — tour
London, Rome, Vienna, Budapest,
return and marry a teacher already morphing
into a mother dwindling to a wife.
To celebrate her new life I decided
she'd use her middle name (which also was
my grandmother's) and love Ulysses. After
about a month, when she rejected Jean
and Joyce and free verse she revised the spelling,
set sail under the banner "Valerie."

While I pursued my studies and she worked
as secretary to Microbiology,
we practiced macrobiology and she
became in action what in principle
she'd been since first we woke up wed and worried,
a mother, and a mother, and another
mother for peace — not just in Vietnam
but anywhere her sons might be called out
to kill — or their only and older sister,
for all that. The bodies of dead birds disturbed
her dreams so deeply she stopped cooking them,
although she hoped some day to have some chickens
scratching in the yard, clucking and laying,
but wouldn't bring herself to eat the eggs,
she said, if ever . . . and the chicks, she feared
would overrun the garden, yard and orchard
she loves to perch in any day she can.

But that was after we had left Seattle,
the University of Adventure, for
life as an archivist for the Mormon Church,

rented a house in Salt Lake — in Rose Park —
and under my father Marden's tutelage
started a garden. Then we moved to Kearns
to a bespoke house and built our own back yard
of sewage sludge and topsoil we bought,
to heal a lot shaved smooth by subdividers.
Here she began another cultivation,
telling the children bedtime stories from
another book she loved, the stories of
destruction, death, a failed civilization,
the austere courage needed to make that record —
Mormon's review of where his people failed.
No sooner had we solved the runoff riddle
anchored the yard with grass, peach trees and veggies
and watched tomatoes sprout from all that sludge
than I changed jobs. We sold, and moved to Orem,
an older house, garden and lawn established,
room for five children and several wives besides.

She kept the books and knew what I was worth
and looked for work, whatever a young mother
could fit in the odd moment. She found room
to work near school as a crossing guard,
stopping traffic, herding kids across
the street — and time to type again for others,
dissertations, curricula vitae
(the closest she'd come to a current curriculum),
letters — but none of that brought any joy.
She found work reading to a blind man, who
appreciated all her education,
challenged her assumptions, called her Mrs.
Clark and taught her much about investment.

So with her wage she bought a bicycle
to stop the car from burning through her dough.
Now we were reading Mormon's book together,
since Meadow could read and Cody was learning how,
before the bedtime stories from *The Hobbit,*
Lord of the Rings, and all the picture books
that passed inspection and were well received
by one and then another of our children,
the last two, born of desert and the valley
ringed with mountains, never had a chance
to miss the cadence of her reading voice.

Ever a gardener, bothered by the waste
of grass, she scalped our yard and set mock orange
to hedge the walk, Wisteria to guard
the door, joining the roses, grapes, and trumpet
vine in making our domicile a jungle,
adding their hues to spring's forsythia,
their scent to all the hybrid scented roses —
and planted the middle yard in flax and flowers,
bearding the house, annoying nosy neighbors
who thought that we should join to make the desert
blossom as a lawn, keep Utah green —
but she preferred the rainbow and perfume
of Eden to the scent of new-mown hay,
and she was far ahead in greening Zion.

Once jealous of two sons who packed and walked
one week along the spine of the Uintas,
Cody and Marden hiking with divers friends
the highest range in the lower Forty-Eight
to run to east and west (and not escape),

she swore the house would not become her tomb.
By now my Scouting trips had turned full-fledged
backpacking, longer, further, deeper, higher,
and as the gear increased so did her lust.
Not one to long for nothing, she planned out
a week-long hike we took with one young son,
Rulon, who'd hated cars for how they turned
the air to gunk, and had to be persuaded
to ride into the mountains with anyone,
leaving our daughter, Meadow, to herd the other
brothers, and using surplus troop external-
frame packs we flew the coop, and after that
did it again, and each time we came back
we found the house too small to hold the sky
we'd breathed, and had to plan to go again.
So Valerie became a gear-head, seeking
lighter and better stuff to fit her frame,
making whatever we couldn't buy or find
so we could go back out into that air.

With summer invited in to tame the house
and all our kids in school, the gardener found
time to divide herself and found more work
halftime, selecting at the library
and buying books across the whole collection —
a garden of weeding at home, a garden of reading
at work — the flower of my profession hers,
helping the readers find and finders read,
a new career she grafted to the root
of all that reading as an English major,
a flowering that filled the public shelves —
while all the basement shelves back in our house

dismayed her as they filled and I built more
to house a private library she found
extravagant, given the City's wealth.

She played *Lord of the Rings* with sons and friends
in a fantasy world of words and dice and rules,
and board games building on our oldest, Scrabble,
enduring evenings of eeeking, farting, belching,
retard-conversing, and the sullen losers
jeered by the brothers who thought they knew the game.
And back in class by now, in Sunday school,
she taught adults what she had learned in years
of reading and retelling the *Book of Mormon*,
so I began to study what she had learned
about the courage it takes to face the death
not of your family only, nor of your town,
nor all your people, but of your civilization.

One winter, to get outdoors, we rented skis
and drove up-canyon looking for a road
closed by the snow where we could practice striding
and falling less, following some instructions
she found in a book she'd bought for the library.
We skidded, slipped and skied along the road
to where it crossed the creek and doubled back
to climb the canyon wall, whence we turned back
and slid and strode and skied our way back down —
enough of a success that we bought skis,
set out cross country in the dead of winter,
survived ski camping, even enjoyed the night
pent in our tent, breath glittering on its walls,
close by our sons and friends who led this trip.

55

Thus we were freed summer and winter, free
to walk the slots of San Rafael Swell,
hike Thousand Lake High Top, and Boulder Top,
back-countries of the state & national parks
and all the trails on all the mountain chains,
where we could live on what we'd carried in
wherever we found us, which was everywhere.
She left me cabling in the Library
and went backpacking in the High Sierra
with just three sons and a hiker friend of theirs
the expedition photographer — I forgave
that choice when she came back a different woman.

The high snows fed a growing interest in
the local flora and ecology —
in Utah, xeriscape. She brought the desert
back, and with a neighbor's help we rigged
a leaky-hose drip trickle irrigation
system that we could pay somebody else's
child to operate while we took our remaining
Anders — the others had left, were leaving, wed,
away at school or on a mission preaching
in foreign tongues in foreign lands — and we
lit out along new paths, the Continental
Divide, a trail like the Pacific Crest,
but further east, in Colorado, and
higher. We found ourselves atop fourteeners
looking down on other climbing hikers
and passed a month amongst the shedding peaks,
the mining districts sad reminder that
men will climb high for gold but leave when beauty
is all they find or when they've scraped together

enough to build a bigger house and settle.
We talked about how everything we did
would strangle us unless we changed direction.

A few years back, still working at the library,
she got a call to herd Relief Society.
It took more energy than she thought she had
so she took up tai chi for self-defense
and meditation, opting for higher reach.
I knew the cost to her of her compassion
but I could see new growth on every limb
and knew another wife was growing, too,
with every visit to her widowed sisters,
to those who'd never married, those who had
and found divorce less painful than endurance,
and those just starting on the path she'd trod,
she's followed, as a mother and a wife.

And now I waken in Ukraine to find
I'm sleeping with a missionary, who
gets up some days before I've gone to sleep
and practices tai chi to keep herself
centered and energized, and keeps her core
in shape with exercises on the floor.
The energy she cultivates she hopes
to spend in service to the people here —
although she yearns for Utah and its snows
and mountain peaks. She wants the time she spends
cooped up in steppes amidst the Russian heart
of yearning for a homeland that betrays
to soothe, her voice to be a Russian balm
to orphaned and abandoned child alike.

My calling is to be a bureaucrat,
keep books, share funds, send rent, chase bills,
    track housing,
but she won't settle for such misery.
Ukraine is not a cross she will shrug off.
When we go walking for a lunch-time break
and climb the street to where the golden-domed
church of the Blessed Vladimir presides
it is a pilgrimage to find the soul
we think Ukraine demands and history
denies. But her concern is not the churches:
the homes have drawn her heart, especially
homes of the homeless, where she hopes to brood
over a bent world, hug it to her breast.

I married many women; no wife of mine
is dead and gone, though some now shine with hope
and some recede into the legends we
concoct to glorify our casual past.
Forty years now I've lived with all these women
and find it true that anyone who has
a library and garden wants for nothing —
except perhaps a shady bench to read on.
I married many women and have learned
to stand as midwife when a new one's born
then stand aside and watch the girl grow.

Golden crown

on a performance by the Georgian National Ballet

If I should die before I leave Ukraine,
toss me into a hole and pile on dirt.
No grave-mound on a ridge for my remains,
no graveyard with the slaughtered and the slain
where conquerors consign the harmed and hurt.

Suppose the next invaders dance above
the mould my bones leave ignorant of my bliss —
what harm, except perhaps to their foot gloves?
Why mark my tomb? — a pride the raiders love —
no crown of mine that any thief would miss.

My flesh will be long gone before my crowns
entice that farmer who ploughs up my teeth,
my jaw and skull incapable of frowns
as cries of joy ring out across the downs
at such fine nuggets in a perfect wreath.

Lies and dreams

How long will I feed myself on lies and dreams
hoping that this time next year I'll be fit
for all the exercises, plans and schemes
I put off now to catch up yesterday?
I have grown fat on nothing — but the play
of appetite across a scrim of reams
of paper holding my holy writ,
now shadows on a monitor of beams.

It lights my cave too far into the night,
illuminating, until I grow numb,
the nightmare that my writing has become,
the terror I reject in holy fright.
Better to sleep and wake without regret.
Best to let lie the horrors of the dead.

INTERLUDE

This Bread, This Water

This bread is sweet upon the tongue
as we employ our fast,
remembering the body hung
on nails till the last.

That body resurrected now
flames with the light of love
warming our flesh with spirit's glow,
brightening Heaven above.

This water washes teeth and lips
that we may speak no guile
but tame the words that form and flip
that glow, for just this while,

that as we testify, we speak
the truth that burns within,
our eyes become a flooding creek
and wash away our sins.

CLOSING EXERCISES

My Father Dwelt in a Tent

My father dwelt in a tent, would not return
to that great city, but sent his sons to retrieve
the plates of brass, God's word, so we could learn —
and back, again, for mates who would believe.

My father dwelt in a tent and waited on God
for further light and knowledge. It came from a tree
he saw in vision, at the head of an iron rod,
protecting pilgrims from filth and mockery.

My Father dwells in a tent; its many stakes
ensure its shade encompasses the Earth.
In every nation, kindred and tongue, it takes
all comers, brings us all to a new birth.

Moroni 12

My father has appeared — not in a dream —
and shown me where to haul the plates off to,
a harder task now that I had the records
of Mormon whole and Ether shortened up,
and needed a bigger box to haul them in —
but I was still accustomed to the pack.
He told me I must take the records off
somewhere the sons of Laman do not live,
but led me back to Akimel Hakathi
to visit with my wife and son, a Kumen,
after the one who married us. I found it
hard to return, and harder yet to leave,
for this was the only family I had known.

I left her once again with child and made
my way with Mormon helping me evade
patrols that Laman sent to trap the few
they could not kill, and so my father, from
his pillar of light appeared and guided me
in wandering to that new and far Cumorah,
north through a waste of rock cut like a corpse,
into high watered valleys — to a dead
sea. Then, guided by a line of peaks,
into the rising sun. The mountains shrank
until I came down to a sea of grass
and sentries where the herds of cumoms feed.

All this was new to me, of forest born.
I moved with care, hunted and marked for death —
and though I found the sites where men would yet

raise temples, there were now no cities there,
and others moved like me. I hid from them,
not knowing how far Laman's sons would seek
to find and kill survivors. I was caught
trying to kill a calf that strayed, with just
my knife, and butcher it. My captors had
no blood of Laman. When they strung me up,
needing to know I was a man like them,
then cut me down, they named me newly theirs.
I wanted to stay, live in a house of skins
and follow the herds across the scroll of seasons,
but I had made a desert river home
and could not tarry where I could become
a bigger target as a stranger here
for anyone who wondered why I'd fled,
what treasure drew me into desolation
and out the other side — richer than fear,
stronger than feud, more wicked than despair.
I could not draw the wolves upon this fold.

I left in greater stealth than I had come
traveling down a river brown with silt
my friends had said would take me to the sea,
with all that soil its flood was bearing off.
This brown earth led me to the red, where God
had fashioned from the dust the first of men
and women. There I left and moved again
across the prairie rolling like a sea
to where my father showed me. There I made
an altar to my God where he would soon,
or late, arrive — not now, but far enough
into the future I could not neglect

the task my father set me, so again
I tracked the river bank to where it joined
a larger, greener river moving slower,
crossed it by night and found a city there
(where on the other shore a river joined),
first one I'd come across. I skirted it,
but lingered too long spying on its mounds
and ramparts. None knew what to make of me.

They made me prisoner, and when they saw
the scars across my chest they made me come
before their king, his war-chief, council chiefs,
and tell the story I had kept concealed,
or die. I'd learned the people's tongue enough
to tell another captive who had come
from that same people in his tongue — but he
knew I was not a warrior of that folk,
and told them I was not his kin. Through him
I told my story, how I'd fled sure death,
a fugitive from Laman and his justice —
the story of two brothers who had fought:
the younger fled, the elder had pursued,
a thousand years, at first just from the shore
to upland, thence into secluded valleys,
and fought more often than they'd loved, for all
those years, till finally like a festering wound,
their civilization split and drenched both tribes
in pus and blood. "No innocent brother's blood
cried from the ground. I only am escaped
alone to tell you. All my people dead —
slaughtered or made betrayers of their own

and only. Some who know me help the sons
of Laman. I have watched them miss my path.

"This is the reason I cannot remain.
I would not willingly expose you to
such hatred. They who follow will proclaim
that you have welcomed death in hosting me
unless there is no trace that I was here."
Such was my plea. They sent me off in stealth
and I have moved in stealth across the land,
living by bow and knife, trading sometimes
with peoples in their camps out hunting meat —
but mostly moving in the shadows, slow,
sleeping in trees, hiding in thickets, caves
that masked my scent, & copses in open country,
not daring to believe I would escape,
led by my father like a liahona
to find this hill whence he would move the plates.
I made this journey to secure the plates
of his and Ether's records, which I'd finished.
So now they're hid across a sea of grass,
and now I have to let it be, and vanish.

I dare not go back to Cumorah now,
and lead the sons of Laman to the records
and sword of Laban, breastplate, lights, perfections —
a treasure they do not know how to value,
or use — except to spend it on their lusts.
I've peeled this bark, write on it with the ash
of fires that I must kindle as I move
through forests that conceal me only half
the year. I have a cave no other man

has found, and leave it when the snows melt off
to make enough to live next winter through,
but will not join my death to any group,
and dare not yet go back to Akimel.
I've seen the sons of Laman in their hunting.

Cut

I think your hair is lovely now
grown just enough
to shade the crest of your high brow
from August sun, and yet allow
light to that bluff.

One curl asserts itself against
its orbit of
an ear, like something too-long fenced,
looking to leave — but, straying, tensed
by counter-love

that anchors it against the sure
humidity
of endless steppe, confined impure
Azovian sea, and breathless shore,
unfree — yet free —

for though your hair holds in the rash
coaxed out
by every new [yet old] hot flash
that burns one strand of brown to ash,
you leave no doubt

you'd rather not one hair be lost —
just off your neck
a bit, and crown your head — not cost
a lot of time to do; the frost
acts as a check.

Head

The way it foams to fill the glass
you know the Coke will lose its head —
its crown subside as seconds pass,
mechanical release of gas.

The membrane of those bubbles shed,
the soda slumps to half its height.
You trickle, so the liquid bled
won't glug — the fizz is still not dead,

but dances like the Prince of Night
leaping above its surface, tense
as Kozaks in a hopak, light
as laughter at another's plight,

and, as you sip, freckles your lenses,
fly-specking the panes of glass
you squint through — proudest of your senses
struggles as this bright air flenses.

Puff of smoke

Let us suppose there is no afterlife.
Our names die with us, as a puff of smoke.
The self we prize subsides into its cells,
electrons cease to race along our nerves,
and like a battery exhausted, brain
refuses to record our images.

What of our marriage then? The dwindling heat
that props me up might seem a petty wage
to anyone who hauls this carcass off
for any work its chemicals might start —
but we've known such joys, my dying breath
will fill the world with viruses of love.

Moroni 13

I never thought to see the hill again.
Two winters had I wandered through this land —
to hide the records one entire year
and back the next — learning the Lamanites
still hunt and slaughter all who, like me, will
never deny Messiah. And I have killed
enough as leader of my own ten thousand
to know the appetite for blood does not
diminish as one feeds it. So I lived
eight year in Akimel, nights with my family,
days in the mountains, searching on both sides
of all the rivers for the most secure
repository for my other tale.

Mormon has bade me in the night to finish
my task. And I have met again the Three
who tarry — they have come to Akimel
and ministered to me. We shared the bread,
and wine from God knows where, as Jesus taught,
and they refreshed my soul with stories of
the days when Jesus walked with them and blessed
the children, how that blessing spread like oil
across the folk and down four generations —
till they could see the people scrub it off
with silks and fine-twined linen, feathered capes
and jaguar skins, with pearls and gold as grit.

They held their goods no more in common, so
they built up churches meaning to get gain,
profaned the sacred, hosted the unworthy

in temples — and imprisoned those who tarried,
whose word rent stone from stone, that they walked free
performing mighty miracles — which failed
to free the hearts of those who witnessed them.

Mormon would have me write the final knowledge
of how we worshipped, even to the end,
and I must move in stealth the sword of Laban,
the liahona, breastplate, and gazelem,
secure them with the other holy records —
and that is why the Three are back again.

They guarded me the day back in Cumorah
it took to finally write as Mormon wanted,
and walked back with me where the ocean sings
and dances in the new year, howling glee —
unlike our journey by the calmer sea,
where people more pacific kept their homes —
by paths they only knew from traveling,
speaking with tribes we met as their own kin,
in tongues they'd had four hundred years to learn,
together and apart. They'd settled once,
learning a local tongue and how to fit
themselves to new societies. They'd wooed
and married and raised children they outlived
and grandchildren who feared them for their youth —
and they know yet the families of their families.

So now they moved as legends on the land
but never family, merchants but not mages,
bringing the knives they fashion out of flint
to trade for food and other local goods,

learned the speech of a hundred different tribes —
a proof they said that God had brought more groups
than ours and Jared's to this goodly land —
and teaching me a few as we moved north.
They taught the ones they'd found had greatest reach
and I'd negotiate our way through cities
not nearly like the Bountiful that died —
but no one asked, their knives drawn back, if we
were Jesus people. And the Three could teach
a little of the love of God to them.

We came into the Mountains-Holding-Clouds,
only a fortnight's travel from the hill,
tracking a bear, a winter's meat for me.
Like and unlike the valleys of my youth
but colder as the days lost light. We chased
this bear because, grown old, it hunted men —
dragging their sleeping children into thickets,
stripping the flesh before the child could wake.
We knew this from the stories people told
of finding their young with faces crushed and flesh
raked from their bones. The tracks told us how old
this bear had grown. Even the shepherd David
might not have found a stone to slay this one!
The people said it was a devil who
could not be killed. They wanted to appease it,
please with the sacrifice of those it slew —
but we had seen the devil and his works
and knew this was an animal that fed.
We tracked it to a cave engulfed in clouds.
Its tracks were glowing as we neared that place,
its scat distinctive — smelled of human flesh

digested, a smell I knew from Sherrizah
and from my peoples' crimes in Morianton.

We kept our arrows nocked as we drew near
watching for sow and cubs in case this king
of peaks had get nearby to feed. He came
up quick and silent from behind, knocked down
one of the Three and flayed him with a swipe
before he turned and stood and got three arrows
to the heart. A second of the Three leapt up
onto its back, hugged it and slit its throat
before it threw him. I hamstrung its leg.
The third drove his flint blade between its ribs
and sliced its heart before that fight was finished.
We skinned it out and smoked its flesh. It might
have been a devil, but its meat was fine.

We took the hide, the hams, the harmed back home
and left the first to heal, the hide to pay —
and half the meat — and struck out for the hill,
living off that beast's hump, cooked as we camped.
We moved north bearing half that ghostly bear,
hanging the meat away from where we slept
in trees no bear could climb — although we feared
the panther more, and moved after we ate,
before we slept. We stayed high on the ridges
letting them point the way till they ran out
and followed rivers north to the long lakes —

the Two spoke of the gouges a great bear
from further north and white as winter peaks
had made with one great swipe of one vast paw,

a tale they'd learned when they sought out the place
to hide the plates, and found a hill like those
built along the greatest of the rivers
they'd traveled, and into its heap of stones
a stone box built to bury the records in,
a barrow for the people of the Lord.

My father has showed me this, his silence proof
enough that I was left alone to finish
the writing of the record of our failure
by seeing how Jared's family had betrayed
itself, God's trust, the promise of this land,
Messiah who would come, and all its children.

The two returned to where the third was healing,
left me to sift through all the hides and bark
for those few bits that still should be preserved
on plates, and having rounded down the record,
bury the plates where they would lie concealed
until a stranger to this story came
whose greed and guile did not exceed his honor,
and I could teach him how to read our speech,
which I have heard none other people use.

Waiting

My daddy died a model death,
my momma's gonna linger;
with every half-remembered breath
she gives ol death the finger.

Not that she wants to stick around;
she's got a jeweled ticker
that only ever makes a sound
when she gulps root beer quicker.

But all those years of eatin good,
livin low on the chicken,
have kept her hummin like she should
and kept her system tickin.

Sometimes she knows she's fit and fly
and goes off for a visit
and leaves a little grin behind:
"I'll just be gone a minute."

But when you look her in the eyes
it's clear that she's not back yet.
This bit bout growin old and wise —
it's jest another racket.

I Dreamed I Saw Joe Smith Last Night

O sane and sacred death

I dreamed I saw Joe Smith last night,
Alive as you or me.
Says I "But Joe, you're decades dead!"
"I never died" says he.
"I never died" says he.

"In Carthage, Joe," says I to him,
a-standing by my bed,
"They framed you on a treason charge."
Says Joe, "But I ain't dead."
Says Joe, "But I ain't dead."

"The State Militia killed you Joe,
they shot you Joe," says I.
"Takes more than guns to kill a man,"
Says Joe; "I didn't die."
Says Joe, "I didn't die."

And talking there as loud as life
And smiling with his mouth
Says Joe "What they can never kill
went on to speak the truth,
went on to speak the truth.

"From Costa Rica to Beijing,
where history meets myth,
where folk of faith are gathering,
it's there you find Joe Smith.
It's there you find Joe Smith!"

I dreamed I saw Joe Smith last night,
alive as you and me.
Says I "But Joe, you're decades dead!"
"I never died" says he,
"I never died" says he.

In this country my prayers
turn into poems

My poems are prayers that I will not succumb
to cynical and jaded views of death.
There is no reason I should not prefer
living to dying, even when my wife
would rather I not touch her with intent
to stoke the fires she would rather quench —
not that she can, or always wants, to kill
the phoenix she thinks finally burned out.

This too is a prayer, a fantasy
I use to feed my faith in our old flesh
that she will sometimes summon the attention
that motion and emotion need to share
in order to rekindle and inflame
the hearth and have the chimney draw again.

I understand the national anthem here:
"Ukraine is not yet dead, her glory not
yet faded" — though she has more fertile soil
than we, and fields that soak up sun and rain
and feed her dreams of self-sufficiency.

I am dependent on that woman who
would be independent, though allied,
and give up habits of fertility —
if only her own provinces did not
betray sometimes the anarchy of lust.

One of my glasses

One of my glasses is always half-full; the other,
half-empty. I look at life from both sides now.
It's one lens of my shades fallen out while I'm driving.
Half the world I see is haloed by dust,
half by the smudge of a finger, or eyebrow cocked.

I wear Coke-bottle glasses; everything
is pinched in at the waist and goblin green:
clearly it's macular degeneration
and tunnel vision, even at second glance.
Now I see through a glass darkly, if at all.

What would it take to half empty a half-full glass?
Think of the surface tension in that tumbler
where two worlds meet, the arid and the moist,
the aqueous and gaseous conjoined —
a little carbonation heals them both.

My wife would nose my glasses as I tongued hers,
after a little accidental affection.
We learned to shed them for any serious kissing,
going in blind and feeling our way around,
and damned if we sometimes don't fall into a ditch.

So I see everything from all sides but
the inside; seems I'm always an outsider
looking in, my nose pressed to the glass,
smudging where I should spray and wipe to get
the single view, not the kaleidoscopic.

Moroni 14

The Lamanites who hunt me now are fewer:
they look for records and relics, not Moroni.
As long as I kept moving across the northlands
where they don't know the languages, and have
no gift of tongues, they moved far slower than I.

These days, these my last days, I live alone,
out of the valley where the rivers run.
The people of the rivers know I'm here,
and we trade, though I grow my own food too,
where waters from the knotted mountains flow,
and visit with my wife and children, nights.

I know my neighbors see me entering
those canyons under heavy load, stay long,
and come out bearing less, a lighter burden.
I make my plans and passages obscure,
and try to lead men through that maze of washes,
defiles and canyons so narrow you can leap
across them at the top, or spider-walk
back down. But then I disappear — as if
the stone had eaten me, or I'd become
one of the pictures pecked into the wall.

I'm far away from Hill Cumorah, hoping
to keep it safe by keeping my scent away.
The sons of Laman hunt me, having heard
that somewhere I'm alive, and have the plates,
the sword of Laban, the ball with its two spindles.
All these I've sealed up and left concealed

far to the east, returning by my first route
through woodlands and their peoples, heavy-laden,
across the grassland where the cows and bulls
move like a cloud of thunder in their dust.

Back into peaks cupping a salted sea
and back along the rivers that feed it still
and those that fed it once. I walked alone,
bearing a heavy load — one under wraps,
staying to learn enough of a language here,
a skill some other place, that I'd be known
to trackers — but still moving across the land,
into a river sunk into the waste,
and out the other side.
         I lived a year
down in that canyon among a people slow
to know and hard to leave. I slept alone
curled around my bundles as if they held
treasure. They were indeed the rock that burns,
and I regaled my hosts with tales of mountains
of such amazing stone. They thought me mad,
but let me heal. I left when I had grown
too fond of them, and climbed back up to desert.
They'd told me of a river in the sand
where people lived who led its waters off
to water maize — that grass that grows in sand —
left over from the giants in the earth,
and beans and squashes, foods I'd learned to love.
I let them think they'd told me some new thing.

Though I have children, those of the Three are dead.
Their children's children's children do not know

the man whose death was watered with the tears
of mother, wife and friends, was laid in stone,
was born again of stone and spirit's flame,
who came to these far isles to feed his other
sheep — they now like wolves amongst the flock
lay waste the fold. They think I too am dead.

These days I live alone, out of the bed
the river runs in. The people of the river
know I live inside the knotted mountains,
and though I visit only in new moons,
my wife's family and friends know I exist.
I know these neighbors see me entering
those canyons under heavy load, stay long,
and come out bearing less. I make my plans
and passages obscure and try to lead
men through that maze of washes, defiles and slots
so narrow you can leap them at the top.
But then I disappear as if the stone
had caught my shadow, painting me at night.

I'm ready. They should come while I still live.
I have some secret places they should find,
where all that weight of rock I bore across
the land could greet them as a falling rain.

Tie one on

Ties are my pantyhose — unnecessary,
constricting, worn only for the appearance
of suavity, something I shed at once
on coming home — and shred, if I'm not wary,
when shredding papers; part of my habit, though.
I'd rather go naked than wear a tie by choice.
But choice of tie is where I find my voice:
black suit, white shirt, black socks, black shoes, but no
black ties, no regimental stripes — pastels,
and floral figures sewn in the silk,
paisley and other patterns of that ilk —
a veritable dependent Book of Kells
bursting with life, the emblem of my Lord
print of his presence, produce of his word.

Rooked

I thought them crows when first they flew on by
last year, outside our windows in Donetsk.
Here in Petrovskii they are streaming next
to dusk, a ribbon of rooks across the sky,

wrapping in pink and rouge the setting sun.
They still won't pose — because I've stopped to focus?
Do they feel stalked, like points inside a locus?
Maybe they think my camera is a gun.

They don't want any attention, steering clear
of one run over in the middle of Bogdana,
stuck to the center stripe, a black banana:
one wing waves in the wind of each passing car.

They don't crave attention; all their talk
is scolding, as it was this bygone fall.
Safer, from higher limbs, calling, if at all,
they croak "awk! awk! awk! Clark!"

POSTLUDE

41st year

I know it's not your favorite thing to do,
cover your clothes with paint over the patching
plaster, cut in tickily around the molding,
squinting to see the light as you are holding
the dripping roller for the next pass, catching
at last the lower sheen, the lighter hue

that shows where you should start, where you rolled last,
where next to hide the old beneath the new.
This house is older than our marriage, though
it's younger by a few years than our bones,
and now that it contains only the two
of us we set about to scrub the past

out of our rooms. We got back from Ukraine,
moved our son out, and found this house was shabby.
Donetsk had shown us how we should proceed —
the garden showed you why with every weed —
the weather proved our insulation flabby —
new windows, and new wiring from the main,

our main resource the money we had saved
by serving in Ukraine, where things were getting
worse as our mission halted to its close.
One president leaves, and everything he knows
leaves with him, the Brethren betting
the next one cannot use a briefing engraved

by fear upon his heart. He sets about
to learn the mission, know the elders, find
where he must renovate and what is sound.

As office couple we inspect the ground,
weed in the lawn — nothing we really mind —
hack at the paving brick that's breaking out

in sand as it reverts to grit and gravel
and welcomes grass and moss — the office floods
not just with paper but sewage, and clean water,
and tears as sisters serve and fight together —
it all speeds up as it slows down, and suds
as thick as fog prepare us for our travel.

When we fly home we're not surprised to find
how little melioration to our house
these eighteen months provided. Now we want
to fix things up by tearing down. Our "remont"
begins almost before we get to grouse.
I'm really glad you hardly seem to mind.

www.ingramcontent.com/pod-product-compliance
Lightning Source LLC
Chambersburg PA
CBHW050014090426
42734CB00020B/3271